MW00614409

A Reason
to Breathe

by Halim A. Flowers

Published by Struggle Against the Odds (S.A.T.O)
3929 Clay Place NE
Washington, D.C. 20019

ISBN 13: 978-0-9778318-0-7

For information regarding permission, write:
S.A.T.O.
3929 Clay Place N.E.
Washington D.C. 20019

Printed in the USA

Second Printing 2007

This book is a reflection of my struggle within these walls. I write from the perspective of a young man isolated from a human life since sixteen. However, being placed in solitary opened me to the universe within and inspired me to live, even amongst the steel bars, barb wire fences, brick walls, gun towers, and life sentences. In spite of everything, this life gives me a reason to breathe.

Dedication

I would like to give special thanks to my Aunt Ruth who encouraged me to read and write. These poems (thoughts) are dedicated to George Jackson, Assata Shakur, Fred Hampton, Harriet Tubman, Che Guevara, and Iyanla Vanzant. They struggled for the better of humanity and gave their dedication, strengths, sacrifices and unselfish love.

Thank you!

I write from you.

CONTENTS

Am I a Menace to Society or
Is Society A Menace to Me?

Americas Juvenile Justice System is filled with contradictions because punitive actions legislated for adults are being imposes upon juveniles. In our society, juveniles are not able to vote or make decisions about their future without the benefit of a legal guardian. Yet, they are subject to the same punitive actions as adult criminals. Ironically, juveniles cannot participate in the election process, which has placed the very people who enact these laws into power because you must be an adult to vote. How can society enforce laws that restrict minors from the benefits adult enjoy except under certain circumstances? If a child is not able to partake in certain activities without a legal guardian, then how does the commission of a certain crime suddenly make them an adult? Americas Juvenile Justice System sends an ambiguous message to our youth – although society sees you as a child you will be punished as a responsible adult.

As I see it, this message encourages society to stigmatize African American youth as menaces. This message reflects our government is out of touch with the environment in which many Americans live. I believe all Americans should share the responsibility to teach our youth how to be of good character just as we all share the responsibility to defend our Country in times of war. We must eradicate this destructive environment that encourages children to commit crimes and become criminals by any and all means necessary.

What could sanction the punishment of a child as an adult? When our laws dictate that minors are not even legally able to manage and function in society. When you imprison children as adults, you can't expect them to become law-abiding citizens. In addition, prisons are not run by people with the best moral character, but individuals who are more prone to ruthless brutality. They are trained to mistreat prisoners' harsh even to the point where they feel very comfortable and justified to assault, humiliate, and murder. How is a man like this delegated the office to correct behavior, when he is in so much need?

We the people of this land fail to correct the factors which enhance the probability of criminal behavior. As a result, there are two million people incarcerated in this country. Instead of laying the blame for this phenomenal on society, where it belongs, we blame minors who are caught up in the system. There should be no surprises about the high rate of recidivism in light of the facts. For one thing, the lack of rehabilitative services in this country and for another the inhumane manner in which prisoners are treated. As an alternative, society chose to believe certain people are born to commit crimes. Perpetuating particular stereotypes, judging and profiling the communities, from which these offenders hail.

(s)
Halim Flowers

A
Reason
to
Breathe

3-16-03

This poem, was inspired by struggle. The female college basketball player who turned her back to the American flag in protest of Armed Forces liberating (Invading) Iraq, was a strong influence for this writing. Also, I make a brief reference to the explosion of the Space Shuttle Columbia.

I love it, I smell it, I breathe it
I see it, touch it, and read it
The struggle, the revolution, the blood
Peace, freedom, and love
All in the air and the people can feel it
Awakened from dreams by the screams of the realist
Rise up sleeping giant and remove your blinders
Run to life cause only death is behind us
Get up and stop being content with crumbs in the belly of the
    beast
The sun will rise in the west all the religious doctors are looking
    from the east
I'm not trying to hear you're not oppressed and your life is
    complete
And then walk past a homeless person in the streets
How could one person live with their self in a mansion
While knowing it's needy children and abandoned orphans in the
    planet
I tried to mourn for fallen space shuttles exploring Mars
But find it hard when everyday I see the innocent die internally
    behind bars
Dropping bombs that leave civilizations to ruins
Imprison me for protecting myself but they get a medal because
    the
President says that they can do it
Because she turned her back to a flag she's not worthy of an
    opinion
What happened to the freedom of speech and expression in this
    land
We live in?
Where was that when crosses were burnt in our lawns

Oh I forgot you separate church from state and the law is dead to
    God
The earth is shaken and protesting your directions
Giving birth to seeds who teethe insurrection

I Walk With Them

This is the first documented poem that I wrote when reading "Blood In My Eyes" by George Jackson. I initially wrote this poem for a spoken word poetry contest that was sponsored by the Moorish Americans. I won second place. But in all actuality, this poem was about myself and all those whose struggled before me.

Though I now exist I walk with the spirit of those before me,
Even though I'm surrounded by this new mentality all can bear
    witness that I'm from the old school of thought,
I was militant with Malcolm X and grew with him to the Malik Al-
    Haij Shabbazz understanding and beyond,
I pounded rock's with axes in bondage for 27 years with Nelson
    Mandela,
And did one more year than that with Geronimo Pratt,
I was isolated 23 hours a day and did 1000 fingertip push-ups in the
    cell with George Jackson in San Quentin,
I took the courtroom hostage with Jonathan Jackson,
I was one of the comrades who liberated Assata from prison,
I was hung from a tree beside Nat Turner,
I wrote the speech that H. Rap Brown delivered in Maryland,
And gave Farrakhan the suggestion to see a million men march,
I marched with Martin below the Dixie line and through the dogs
    and hoses,
I fought along with Hannibal in the Swiss Alps,
I help organize the blueprint for the economic revolution with
    Marcus Garvey,
When the California Supreme Court reversed his conviction I was
    the one who took Huey P. Newtons picture when he was on
    top of the car with his shirt ripped off,
I've killed the lion with my bare hands to have the honor to fight
    under the banner of the Zulu warriors under the command of
    Shaka,
I was one of the eleven who survived the ambush on the Cuban
    shores with Castro from Mexico and fought guerilla warfare
    with him in the mountains outside of Havana,

Then removed the dove from his shoulder when he gave his
    speech when he first came to power,
Then I convinced Che Guevera to leave his high position in Cuba
    and we gave our life for the revolution of the Bolivians,
My thoughts are with them and their sacrifices were done with the
    image of me in their mind,
I see them, hear them, talk with them, debate with them, feel
    them, touch them,
The Jordan's, Tyson's, Pryor's, and Jackson's are not my walking
    partners,
I'm not bred from the genetics of the entertainers,
But revolutionists who insurrect courage and self-sacrifice against
    inner-fear,
We know no sacrifice too big for the sake of justice for our people,
We hate life if it doesn't present a cause to suffer and die for,
To walk with us is to walk with death,
To walk with death is to walk with no fear,
To walk with no fear is to walk with true life,
I walk with them.

The Petting Zoo

I wrote this in honor of all the beautiful, strong, and loyal women who took the time to write, accept the call, or visit a brother held captive. I would like to let the Queens know that their contributions are vital to the brother's sanity and that they are extremely appreciated.

He waits patiently in his cage,
Waiting for that touch that brings peace,
The pet that erases isolation and makes him forget the distance in
    between the last pet,
She writes him her thoughts,
She pets him!
He analyzes her emotions and being thrilled by her pet stiffens,
She blesses him with the pleasure to hear her thoughts,
She pets him!
Her voice tranquilizes him like the cat when it's fur is rubbed,
Upon hearing her words he thanks God for installing the thought
    to invent the telephone,
No one in the zoo possesses her potent sound,
So to hear her is an unusual sound than what's normally heard in
    the zoo,
He closes his eyes, stuck, he rubs his hands on the phone like the
    cat on it's massagers legs
She visits him,
She Pets him!
Like a puppy in a pound, he longs for her to take him home with
    her,
He hugs her and her softness brings pleasure and pain,
Elated to be shrouded by her presence,
But the prospect of her departure makes her lion whine internally
    for the master of the desires of his soul,
Her kiss brings him back to reality,
Her hand upon his,
She Pets him!
And they converse, plan, strategize,
He watches her leave,
Her walk, her hair, her curves, her strength,

Gone from his gaze,
He mourns!
But she has brung hope,
Her pets produces smiles and contains a powerful force that emits
    energy,
The zoo is his world,
His existence,
She visits his conscious in many ways,
And pets him!!

Love Birds

One day I was locked down in a cell and I looked out of the window and watched two birds enjoy love. The act was so natural and peaceful, that my being denied to experience that expression enticed envy. What was amazing to me was the consistency and intensity of the seduction because it lasted for over a hour.

One day I layed in a cage and outside the window I saw two
         pigeons,
Instantly I could sense that one was a male and the other his
         queen,
His chest puffed-up,
And she possessed that feminine posture that all females are
         blessed with,
Even Birds!
On the ledge of a building they sat there that hot summer day in
         August,
Cuddling, fondling, and kissing,
Amazed I watched as she rested her head on his chest,
And how he caressed the top of her head with passionate strokes,
At the time when the heat of the sun and humidity would force
         other creatures to remain apart and to rest in the cool
         of the shade,
These two love birds went at it for hours in the public like attention
         craved exhibitionist,
I watched them from my cage for over a hour,
They were free and enjoying the liberties of love and peace that all
         creatures deserve,
As they smothered each other they occasionally glanced in the cage
         at me,
As if they were teasing me,
But I wondered if The God sent them to inspire me,
And to remind me of the human rights that even the animals
         enjoy.

I'm Angry

I wrote this poem for all women in a traumatic relationship. My heart especially goes out to the young women in my family. Basically, this expresses my feeling for women that accepted stagnation and depression in the place of loneliness. I'm angry, you picked this poison!

I'm angry!
Tired of being held captive from the triangle of my pleasures in
    breathing,
Family, Women, And Freedom!
But nevertheless I hope,
I hope when others foresight could only forecast grief and defeat,
Me myself,
I see a challenge and a battle of the wills,
I'm angry that our women have forgotten how to be loved,
So they accept that individual who possesses the opposite of her
    genitalia,
Whose limbs have reached their zenith of development,
And now proudly says, "I'm a man",
Meanwhile he patrols and dictates her adobe without assisting his
    finances for it's maintaining,
Slaps her, beats her, and even places his walking utensils upon her
    womb,
Swollen with life from his semen,
In the presence of their own child,
And when her friends ask her why she tolerates his tantrums,
Her answer is "I love him",
Naturally they call her stupid,
But I know that she loves stronger than iron,
And is blinded by the often repeated inner voice that soothes her
    bruises when it whispers,
"He'll change",
My sisters who are faced with this tragedy,
As you watch the object of your merciful affection,
With his right hand on the remote,
Left hand in his crouch,
Sitting on the couch with his feet on the table,

Barking orders for you to retrieve beverages,
As you read this,
Know that you have one pious, peaceful, and angry brother in this
    world,
Who possesses the fury and pleasure to grab him by his collar,
And headbutt him in his nose,
And throw him from your furniture through a closed glass window,
With bars on it's perimeter,
I'm angry right now.

How Pretty You Are

While I was in solitary confinement, I envisioned the singer Ashanti as my wife. In the vision, we made love and she became pregnant. When she was about to deliver the child, I kneeled down and recited this poem about our daughter named Sakheena. In Arabic it means "tranquility" Deep vision, huh!

I wrote this to inform you on how pretty you are,
So that you won't think that I forgot how pretty you are,
I watch you from a distance and think how pretty you are,
Thinking maybe you don't know how pretty you are,
I sit and watch you read and think God how pretty you are,
Something about your sideburns how pretty you are,
Lay in your lap and look in your eyes how pretty you are,
Even when your mad damn how pretty you are,
If they could witness your naked flesh they would know how pretty
    you are,
Even with the headwrap, cloak and veil they can still smell how
    pretty you are,
The way you received my seed shows how pretty you are,
And when your face and stomach got fat and toes and feet swollen
    its amazing still how pretty you are,
When I saw you sweat and scream, the womb stretched to make way
    for life I almost forgot how pretty you are,
But when you first held our child and smiled I remembered how
    pretty you are,
Every stretch mark attest that you sacrificed your flesh and how
    pretty you are,
To the end of my days I want to let you know how pretty you are,
Turn over in my grave to say how pretty you are,
On the day we are raised I'll proclaim how pretty you are,
Dreds, ponytail, or gelled hair don't change how pretty you are,
Even the simplest braids can't shade how pretty you are,
People could get paid to take pictures of how pretty you are,
If I wasn't so jealous I'd allow my comrades to say how pretty you are,
So hopefully it'll suffice for me, myself, and I to say,
    How pretty you are.

Find Her

I dedicate this poem to all of the strong Afrikan woman who represented with courage and loyalty. I believe that spirit resides within all women but some are ignoring it or are destined to be presented with a situation, predicament, or person to awaken it within them. Also, I have a deep and lethal admiration and crush with that spirit within the woman.

Who can find one whose words guides a prince to Kingship,
Whose poems arouse erections and inspires insurrection,
Her speech produces sound-waves of energy that revolutionizes the
    mind,
Her smile strengthens the heart and tenses the testicles,
As clever as Hatshepshut,
Governs with justice like Nefertiti,
Overlooks and forgives like Coretta Scott King,
Handles separation and bondage with patience like Winnie
    Mandela,
And will risk her being to free others as Harriet Tubman,
Who'll leave so much to pursue freedom like Assata Shakur,
Intelligent and eloquent as Angela Davis,
Speaks out against oppression and injustice like Sojourner Truth,
With a pur as salacious as Eartha Kitt,
But as chaste as Betty Shabazz,
Doesn't desire the riches of Oprah,
But the virtues of wisdom,
Great men desire her presence like the Queen of Sheba,
Her touch brings tingles,
Her womb is a healing,
Her breasts bears sustenance,
Under her feet is paradise,
Her lap is the essential university of all humanity,
What the queen is to the hive is what she is to the earth,
Where can one find this one of a kind?
If you find her let her know she's created to mate with the soul of
    men who possess the stature of mine...

Images In The Water

This is a message to the thugs, drug dealers, the narcotic and alcoholic abusers. Love is strange.

Just because you've sold drugs does that make you a thug?
If so, the CIA does it also, are they thugs?
Just because you've killed someone does that make you a killer that
    deserves glory?
Do you have an aphrodisiac for being feared?
You say that you fear nothing but God but when your babysitters in
    blue appear you run
Is it their guns you fear?
Don't you have an AK-47?
Do you sell drugs because your starving or have you taken it up as a
    hobby to support your other hobbies of fashion and vain?
Getting intoxicated makes you feel good
Do you feel bad when you are sober?
Is reality that low and dry that you have to get high and drunk?
You say that you love yourself but intake substances into your body
    that you know will destroy you
Is it healthy for you to love someone else?
You're incarcerated and proclaim boastfully "I'm A Man"
Do you know that the 13th Amendment of the Constitution says
    that a convicted felon is subject to involuntary servitude and
    slavery
And the U.S. Supreme Court once said that a slave is 3/5 of a
    human being?
So, when you're imprisoned you relinquish some of your human
    rights
Doesn't that equate you with animals?
And all you outlaws in society who purchase consumer products
    and pay taxes that support the prisons that you say you hate
    because they contain your Homies
If you are paying aren't you being extorted?
Doesn't that make you a coward?

Halim A. Flowers

I-E-A-L-J-S

*One night I had a dream about India Arie and I decided to write a missive
explaining how much I adore India Arie, Erykah Badu, Angie Stone,
Lauryn Hill, Jill Scott, and Sade. Truly, their voices have calmed the souls
of many brothers held captive. I've had some vivid dreams in which India
Arie and I engaged in stimulating dialogue. Maybe our antennae are
frequenting the same consciousness. Anyway, on behalf of so many
brothers, I sincerely appreciate the songs that you sisters have sing to our
souls.*

I've spoken to you in my dreams,
Your melodies have danced upon my soul to the extent that you
      prey upon my unconscious,
Let me talk with you,
Then guitar in hand inform me on how Stevie has inspired you,
Make me feel beautiful and proud about my brown skin and how
      you're not the average girl whose wealth is not determined by
      monotonous attire,
Mother of seven,
Tell me why your eyes are green and why I shouldn't let them
      name no Structure after me,
Please don't stop,
Go on and on and on,
If paradise is all I can imagine then I'll see you next lifetime,
If not sight then at least hear you,
Every sun needs the comforting sight of the orange moon,
How good it is,
Ms. Mahoghany,
Precious stone,
Uplift me, Make me feel what I am,
Unique, strong, and royal,
Tell us how you love those with profession and even the ones held
      captive,
You love us all,
I know that they hated those tunes,
Even remixed the tempo,
That's right sport that afro,

We love you sister comrade,
Rise out of those tranquilizing Carribean hills Ms. New Jerusalem
     and perform for me one last encore,
Let me hear your love for the Zion,
How we're mostly about that thing,
And how they know not what they do,
Remind me of the sweetest thing known likened to the lips on the
     collarbone,
That feeling that makes nothing even matter no more,
Tell me it'll be alright,
The princess of the city of love,
I need some love to rain down on me,
As we take a walk in the park,
Looking at the stars pondering surahs,
Amazed by the revelations,
I know their watching me,
Cook, clean, provide, and protect,
Yes that is the way I love you baby,
The queen of them all,
Captor of my consciousness,
Perpetual sound in my heart,
The surgeon for my loneliness,
A smooth operator,
Take off your shoes and tell me how my love is king,
The voice of utopia,
This can't be an ordinary love,
Take me to meet the woman in Somalia,
Tell me about Jezebel,
When drowning in despair,
Your notes prove to be the rock for the lovers to cling to in the
     ocean of isolation,
I'll cherish the day that I hear you all,
Truly a love deluxe,
Ladies of love,
Ladies of my life...

                                                  Halim A. Flowers

EVOL

Evol is love spelled opposite. Why? I've never had a female besides my mother to showed me sincere and unconditional love like my Queen Stephanie. Our relationship is very unconventional, due to my imprisonment. Nevertheless, she finds a way to tolerate me. How many women would invest that level of energy in a man serving forty plus years? Deep!

I often wish that I could touch her skin as I have caressed her
    heart,
Rub and massage through the strands of her hair like I've soothed
    her mind and soul,
When consumed with despair,
Feeling weak, distorted, and unwanted is how she came to me,
I saw salaciousness in sincerity and attraction in piety,
So I convinced her of the uniqueness of the shades of beauty that
    she overlooked in the mirror,
Still we have barriers mentally, physically, and spiritually,
She see's three light's of deification,
While the tunnels of my comprehension vision's One,
Barriers of isolation and illness,
Feeling sometimes like why has The God put us through this,
Not that we're discontent but wondering why the testes are so
      heavy and in the end what will be the wise meaning to all of
      these struggle's,
She taught me that love is more than visible and physical senses,
But a light and energy that is unseen and untouchable,
Which penetrates through steel, brick walls, gates, phones, bars,
    ink, trees, and lead,
It knows no distance,
Connected to the soul,
Manifested in deeds,
Expressed through sex,
Which produces life,
Power.

To See You Loved

This is another poem, I wrote about Stephanie. Letting her know, I will always cherish her even if she moves on.

I would love to see you loved,
I hurt to see you deprived of it,
We all need it,
Some of us have it,
Only a few of us are deserving of it,
Don't want to see you wait for a love that may not be allotted your
    fate,
It would be selfish of me to not want to see you loved,
Even though it may not be a share of my lot to provide you with
    love,
I love you enough to see you grow,
Love is like the sun,
Every earth is dependent upon it's nurturing,
Wouldn't want to see you stagnated,
Grow my love,
Report to me how it feels to grow,
I've been stunted for years,
Shrouded by the weeds of separation,
Isolated from light, from love, from cultivating and grazing upon
    growth,
Why would I want to see you dwarfed?
Grow in the undefinable mystery of love,
You're so fertile, fresh, and green,
But without love,
Blue as the grass in Kentucky fields,
I would love to see you get a peace of love,
I would love to see you loved...

There Is A Spirit Between The Covers

After reading some of George Jackson works, I wrote this about him. I recommend all Afrikan descent males read George Jackson.

When others just saw two covers with sheets in Between them with
    words, I felt a spirit,
That inspired me to condition every limb on my body,
To train more strenuously than the common human being,
Push-ups upside down and on the tips of my fingers and knuckles,
Practice my kicks and master my headbutt,
Prepare to use my entire body as a weapon,
A spirit that guided me to study the truth,
Study until my brain hurt,
Study until I despise Studying,
And still keep studying,
A spirit that motivated me to be a student and teacher of the
    people,
And taught me that to teach the people you must first be their
    student,
Enlightened me to the fact that to study the people is to know the
    people,
To know the people is to feel the people,
To feel the people is to be one with the people,
To be one with the people is to be properly prepared to die for the
    people,
A spirit that instructed me to spread the truth to all who are worthy
    of being exposed to it's infection,
A spirit that made me enjoy the hidden benefits of isolation and
    separation,
And to withstand with honor and dignity any oppressive tactics that
    the pigs provided for me,
To appear to even enjoy them so they could never see me sweat,
A spirit that encouraged me to despise fiction and to become and
    associate with realist,
A spirit that increased my passion and respect for women and
    freedom,
A spirit that convinced me to be an advocate for human rights and
    made me conscious of what they are,

A spirit that made me understand the blessings of a sacrificial
    death,
And that the spirit of truth will be heard and felt forever,
Live on Comrade George...

Time For Reflection

I wrote this for the birthday of my other mother, "Pup". But it is a maxim for anyone blessed enough to experience living another Birthday.

A day to reflect on our growth,
How each year we become new,
To learn and acquire new knowledge makes us fresh and young,
The flesh originates from the earth that's been walked upon for
    centuries,
So in skin reality,
The bare fact that we are born old is the naked truth,
But our minds were clear and pure,
Unable to emit and interpret any dialects or languages,
So this day we reflect on our growth from then to now,
The many experiences in life that the mystery of time has
    presented to us,
The highway of choices and the paths we chose,
The roads that were rocky were full of holes that became parables
    of wisdom,
Which produced many inner untold adage,
And the smooth pavements were installed into our conscious as
    memories that enlighten our hearts and give us a reason to
    breathe,
Mountains were climbed that were unavoidable for us to escape the
    unbearable task of completing the expedition of seeing what
    was waiting for us on the other side of them,
To make us aware of the virtues that we couldn't see that we
    possessed,
And oceans were split in half for us to walk through to make us
    believe that we were worthy of miracles,
To commemorate this day we have precious stones from the earth,
Horoscopes from the astronomical signs in the heavens,
And celebrations, feasts, and receiving of gifts,
But in the midst of those distractions,
Remember to Reflect,
Happy Birthday.

WHY

I wrote this about a family member who betrayed me.

I wonder if you knew that you were destroying a foundation of trust
    that was built up for years?
Connected by blood,
While you were committing that act of treachery,
Did you know the consequences would be the lost of all respect
    from one who placed your betraying life before his own?
Remember when we were on the edge of the bridge between life
    and death?
And I pleaded, begged and even cursed at them to make sure that
    you were safe before they touched me,
To get you to safety first,
I was willing to die a young death for your betraying soul,
Did you remember that when you looked at the faces of the dead
    presidents on the paper
Currency that you received?
I wanted to die for you,
You said that you did it for money when I asked, "Why?"
If it was that bad I would've robbed a bank for you,
Or even robbed him,
That would've been menial for one who tried to die for you,
So that is why I never accepted your excuses,
The best you could've done was never told a soul,
But you slipped and I caught your deceptions,
How could you lay with him when he was trying to kill me?
I'm your blood,
He was trying to shed it,
You betrayed all those who cherish my blood and my life,
It is that same blood that prevented me from shedding yours,
I bet that you never knew that I wanted to take your life,
Since I tried to give mines for yours I felt justified,
But when I saw you I saw me,
When your lover died and you told me,
I laughed so hard in your face just to make you feel like trash,
Remember that?

            Halim A. Flowers

But when I lost my close comrade who beared your alias,
You didn't laugh,
But grieved with me,
That was the day I forgave,
Maybe my defense mechanisms were weakened by tragedy,
I dropped my guard and let you in,
But when you became occupied by another life within your womb,
I could no longer find it in myself to hate you,
Your child played a vital role in my acceptance of you,
So every time I see that child,
I smile,
Because that child is a manifestation of my forgiveness and love for
    you,
I forgave but never forgot,
You shouldn't either,
Deceiving people who would die a young death for you could be
    detrimental,
Everyone isn't strong enough to forgive,
Cherish your life,
I'm honest when I say, "I forgive, I love you",
But I still want to know "Why?"

Can't Escape That Feeling

This is a poem that attempts to illustrate the many different experiences of tribulations that everyone will face. Instead of despising the emotions that are produced by our trials, we should learn ourselves, gain the wisdom behind why we feel that way, and understand that in order to know strength, it must be presented opportunities to be applied.

17 years old and sentenced to life in prison,
Now he must except books, exercising, and religion in the place of
      drugs, women and fast living,
Can't escape that feeling,
A rose that blossomed with thorns of her father molesting her
      engraved in her brain,
But her blissful life of matrimony with her husband and daughter
      erases the pain,
She returns home from work early one night to be greeted at the
      door with sounds of holler's and screams,
Rushes upstairs to her daughter's room only to find her spouse
      sweating in between their daughters womb with the eyes of a
      crazed sex phene,
Can't escape that feeling,
A happy couple sends their innocent daughter off to college,
Left a virgin but now studies boys instead of knowledge,
Her parents start to think they've made a mistake when she flunks
      her first two semesters and then comes home for spring break
      pregnant,
Only to have the doctors tell her she is HIV positive,
Now her parents really regret it,
Can't escape that feeling,
A single mother, independent, strong, raised her only son with
      morals and all that he wanted and could ever have,
Almost fainted when he told everyone at Christmas dinner that
      he's in love with another man,
Can't escape that feeling,
Remember that 17 year old,
He's almost 30, won his appeal and upon his release,
Family members faces grief he meets because a pedophile has

kidnaped, raped and molested his niece,
Why can't he escape that feeling?
The night of their 50th anniversary she tells her husband that she
can't bear the guilt anymore as they walk in their bedroom
door,
I've been building up the courage for 48 years to inform you that
Junior's not yours,
Can't escape that feeling,
Raised in a fortune 500 company owning family who lived life like
money grew on trees,
He always was able to receive all the wants that his sight could see,
Now he's CEO and founder of his own Fortune 500 company thats
hit with an accounting and tax scandal on the verge of
pursuing Chapter 11 and broke,
He decides to bow out gracefully with a bottle of pills, a glass of
water and a suicide note,
Still can't escape that feeling,
He was incarcerated for a decade to return to the death of his
niece,
Wondering did the appellate court reverse his conviction with the
foresight of this grief,
Sick of being indoors on his first night home he decides to take a
walk to the corner store,
The last words he heard was, "Remember Me", his last sight was a
barrel as his bullet riddled, book smart, healthy, religious, and
lifeless body hit the floor,
And his last thought was, can't escape that feeling,
That feeling we associate with pain,
No matter how many times it hurts the same,
That feeling that has a place in everyone fate,
If you think you're too righteous so you'll escape,
Watch and wait,
That feeling is there to make us stronger,
And to remind us that this life is short and the state in the grave is
longer,
So it don't matter if you reside on the surface of the deepest ocean
or climb to the top of the highest building,
It's simply impossible to explain and escape that feeling...

Dream Lover

This poem is a blueprint for my perfect woman. After all, this is just my fantasy!

She is an artist,
She is a work of art,
The wrappings of her crown represents wisdom,
She has been liposucted from deifying material substance,
Her cooking is food for the soul,
I watch her in the garden clipping weeds, watering roots, waving at
    flies, smelling pedals, and singing to plants,
She is dedicated to the earth,
Submissive to The Creator,
Everything in the heavens and the earth has been made
    subservient to her,
The youth of the city congregate to her dwelling to hear her read
    the stories of history of the prophets, the sincere, and those
    who sacrificed their lives and all those who were good for
    humanity,
Her doors are never closed to the hungry,
Her food is for the village,
All the children on the block can smell to come by when she's
    fixing pie,
Her breasts stays filled with milk for her offspring that never runs
    dry,
Her body is amazing,
That only her husband will know,
Tickles with her tongue,
Coke bottle hips,
And controls muscles that coerces tears from the eyes of her
    prince,
She is in tune with the elements and enjoys simple things,
Like flying kites, watching stars, cool nights laying embraced with
    me in blankets on the shore of the river listening to music and
    reciting poetry,
And smiling,
She is the soother of my soul and the product of my beautiful

imagination,
Every exercise that I've done,
And the choice to discipline my consumption to a healthy diet was
done to preserve my physique to be attractive and delicious
for her,
I love her,
And with the thought of pleasing her,
I have a reason to breathe.

Hide And Seek

I wrote this poem specifically to my young sister Angie. A young lady with all the potential to elevate herself to be the envy of queens. I think that sometimes we can't comprehend how unique and extraordinary we are. Wake up everyone and stop being common. Life is to ever changing to be normal.

There is something hiding in you that I seek,
Something irresistible hidden in you that I see,
Right up under your nose but you can't comprehend it's fragrance,
Senses blocked by frivilous amusements and destructive habits,
Your ship contains a grand spirit,
That's been navigated by a distorted compass,
Directions that were original became obsolete,
Lost the vision of returning east to chasing a north star,
Running from the lion to the cave of the bear,
To be spoiled is void and caring is strength,
I wont accept that you're selfishly weak,
Enshrouded with potential that only the microscopic eye of the
      savant can see,
Only the cretins need a magnifying glass to grasp that you've got it,
I could help you see it if you close your eyes and be still,
Be silent and listen to the destiny of inner-visions,
Don't peek-a-boo with potential and lose all sight,
And play hide and seek with greatness for the rest of your life.

Halim A. Flowers

Pharaoh's Passage

My intent for writing this was to remind my mother that all sages are always placed under confinement or attempts of assassinations by the oppressors of that time. So, she should expect and accept with dignity my perils.

As others were sending their son's off to college and the military,
To get a common education,
Common training,
A common job,
To live a common life and die a common death,
In which they were never really living because their presence was
    the norm,
And they never grasped or emitted that eternal and unforgettable
    revolutionizing energy called truth,
You were preparing to place your beloved prince in the basket to
    sail down the purging River of adversity and tribulation,
Leading to the palace of Pharaoh to escape the murderous mental
    death of conforming to the unjust and oppressive traditions,
And to be purified by the trials of captivity which presented it's
    torments of isolation and separation,
Which was essential for the process of breeding a man-child savior,
Who'll resurrect the breathing cretins from their slumber,
Those who rest in rose petal mattresses of lethargy and torpidity,
Understand that all of the sages trod this path of affliction to
    become bludgeoned by the edge of the common misguided
    people's nihility,
In order to become rectified with the remedy of discernment and
    valiance,
Know that you sent your son towards his destined direction to be
    remembered in the Annals of history as one of the eminent
    reformist who challenged deceiving cannon and frivolous
    customs,
With this aphorism know that the future scholars will reflect that
    behind every savant man was a stronger mother...

Sobriety Test

This is a reality check to everyone who can't explain the reasons why they intoxicate themselves. Only a insane person does things without knowledge of why he or she does that particular act. This is a test to see why being sober seems so uncomfortable to some people.

I'm drunk off water and high off living,
The only thing that I'm inhaling from trees is oxygen,
Why waste sour grapes for celebrations when I can eat them fresh,
Don't need to induce any substances to feel good,
I don't feel bad sober,
The only thing I'm putting in papers is thoughts,
I'm spaced out on seeing the moon and stars,
Intoxicated by inner peace,
Why would you want to distort your thoughts?
Do you wake up not wanting to think?
Are conditions that bad to make you try to escape reality?
So you just alter your mind to handle the truth.

Dependant

I wrote this to inform people on how the beauty of things are dependent upon another. We should appreciate whatever it may be that enhances our illumination. To devalue that X-Factor would be equivalent to debasing ourselves.

The night without stars,
Humans with no trees,
The church, mosque, and synagogue with no congregation,
Guns with no ammunition,
Prisons with no captives,
A poet with no means to scribe,
A performer with no audience,
A dictator with no one to oppress,
A plantation with no slaves,
A revolutionist with no cause,
A singer with no one to listen,
An author with no readers,
A man with no woman,
Birds with no sky,
Fish with no oceans,
A script with no actors,
Sex with no orgasms,
A vision with no mission,
A Shepard with no flocks,
A mathematician with no numbers,
The earth with no sun,
The spring with no green,
The teacher with no students,
The predator with no prey,
The gifts with no one to give them to,
The morning with no chirping of birds,
The day with no light,
The thought with no words,

We all need someone, someplace, or something to bring out the
    best in us,
Without it we would have no meaning, no purpose, no splendor,
Cherish whatever it may be for you and be grateful that it is there.

With Me

This is a list of actions that I desire for my Queen to partake in with me. I think that in order for a man to sustain a genuine foundation with a woman for decades, the very essence of their companionship, he must relay to her the morals and characteristics that he expects for her to emit, so that her radiance will remain pleasing to his consciousness.

Fast this month with me,
Liberate my ikhwan and blast with me,
Read these books with me,
Debate with me,
Learn this part of the Qur'an with me,
Make love with me,
Make love to me,
Put your head on this sand and pray with me,
Visit this sacred land hold hands and hajj with me,
Give life to this seed with me,
Breathe with me,
Get on your knees and plead to the Creator with me,
Stay with me,
Even in the grave lay with me,
Don't play with me,
Feed the poor with me,
Take care of home when the opposition war with me,
See the world and tour with me,
Lay naked on this persian rug floor with me,
Never bore with me,
When I'm too low never walk in the pit with me,
But pull me up and when I get too high don't become arrogant
     and conceited with me,
Be level with me,
Never do wrong with me,
Never fear to sacrifice your life for what is right with me,
See my right hand hold it with me,
Take these perpetual vows with me,
Tolerate this life, the grave and the hereafter with me,
Hold me and pluck snot out our babies nose with me,

Teach with me,
Speak with me,
Train with me,
Consume veggie and grains with me,
Stand by my side with me,
When the odds are stacked ride with me,
Cry with me,
Learn with me,
Be stern with me,
Be kind with me,
Do you have the courage to live with me???

Halim A. Flowers

He Is

Simply stated, this writing is a manifestation of everything I am and strive to become.

He is who he is,
He is the forgotten prince,
The champion for the oppressed,
The provider for the poor,
The shelter and guardian of orphans,
When he has to protect himself, his family, and comrades,
Yes, he is a murderer,
He is a sage,
He is the student and teacher of the people,
His quotes are adage,
His jokes are aphoristic,
He is the servant of Wisdom,
He is hungry .for knowledge,
He is water for the malnourished minds,
He is the darling of the queens,
The desire of the princesses,
He is a sight to see,
His forehead bears the mark of submission,
His eyes are brown,
His lips are pink,
His smile is handsome,
His chest is firm,
His stomach is like rocks,
His biceps are like baseballs,
He is hung,
His calfs are like bricks,
He is a living proverb,
He has been instructed and raised by the lessons of history,
He has been purged in the fire of isolation and separation,
He maintains his cool composure throughout his purging,
Now he is stronger,
He is light to the dead,
He inspires the poets,

He is the love of his mother,
The pride of his father,
What the pious seek for a husband,
What every child needs for a father,
Honorer of the rights of his sisters and brothers,
He is not perfect,
He is the embodiment of the spirits of the sincere sacrificer's,
He is who he is,
He is I.

Her Beauty

This was scripted in reference to the demagogue we have come to identify as Amerika. Detailing some of her many imperfections that she somehow overlooks. Sometimes we can't perceive any defects besides the ones that we see in others.

Whatever she touches she makes pure;
Ms. Moraliser of Humanity,
She only wants the people of the earth to be freed by
        democracizing them with
Capitalistic liberties,
What has it done for her?
The land of the free,
With the most people on earth held captive,
The home of the brave,
Where the soldiers fight wars hundreds of miles in the sky,
Rarely man to man
A coalition with her against one isolated place equivalent to one of
        her states,
The land of the freedom to be a pedophile predatorial priest
Corporation crook or to ambush an establishment of business with
        bullets because of despair,
A land of peace,
More like a war zone,
From her rural,
To her suburban,
To her urban,
One where the confused child kills his parents and siblings,
The other disturbed adolescent rampages his school with
        ammunition,
And the other where the youth murder at a higher rate than
        anywhere else in the world,
Not even your children are innocent anymore,
The land of the free,
Sort of like a police state,
Not many places on earth occupy non-military officers to babysit
        their society with arms,

But you're one of them,
The land of opportunity,
The rich get richer and the poor pay more taxes
The wealthiest land on the earth,
With some of the most unsanitized ghettos
Homeless laying in the big city streets,
Veterans sleep on your concrete,
Elders eat pet food to purchase your inflated prices of medication,
Citizens are refused care because of insufficient funds for coverage,
Condemner of dictators human rights
Have you visited some of your prisons,
Where officers correct humans by beating them with boots, clubs,
    shocking them with shields, stunning them with volts,
    strapping them with four point restraints so they can starve
    them and watch them urinate and defecate on themselves and
    spray them with hoses,
Have you overlooked how the police beat, plunge objects in the
    rectum, and shoot unarmed citizens,
Lady of liberty,
Where is the love in this land?
You've portrayed and paraded your women as flesh,
So your men don't respect them and vice-versa,
Result is the highest divorce rate in existence;
The women would rather be artificially inseminated,
Women lust women and your men lust men,
You're so unnatural,
I don't even know why you're described in the feminine,
You don't possess any of the nurturing and merciful traits of the
    woman,
Remember your military base was attacked and you retaliated by
    destroying civilians and their land for decades,
You know that the trees are our source of breath and you still
    destroy them,
Pollute the air and water with hazardous toxins,
You are a brute, You are a beast,
You are Amerika!

Halim A. Flowers

Matrimonial Moment

I wrote this as an offset to a poem that my oracle Anissa wrote me titled "Sticky." I believe that sexual relations must be in accord with the divine that is why I named this piece "Matrimonial Moment" for its sexual content and energy.

I''m ailing with the separation from your salaciousness,
My head is full of phelgm,
I've already told you that your womb is a healing,
My being deprived of it has left me dehydrated and malnourished,
Your breasts are the bearers of sustenance,
My body is so hard, stiff, and straight,
Yours is totally opposite,
Soft, smooth, and curvacious,
Yet I enjoy pleasure,
You encourage my implying a little pain,
Let me french kiss your uterus and massage in between your thighs
     with the liquid that is produced by climaxation,
Since my seeds paradise is beneath your feet,
Stand upon my abdomen,
As I tense to bear the pressure of your weight,
To you it feels as if your toes are walking on hard rocks of coal,
Ease upon me,
Upon entrance I'm left alone with your iris,
The color of the dove,
This image brings me peace,
Tell the back of your skull to share the view of your elegant pupils
     with me,
Let me gaze at the mirror of your soul and pinch your tips,
They feel as hard as the texture of raw diamonds,
Turn around so that I'll surprise you,
I don't want you to absorb my distorted face when I come,
As I cultivate the earth let me sink my molars into your neck like
     the lion,
Sun upon Earth,
With this mixture of waters,
Lets make life.

Bitter Weeds

A message to all human beings, especially people who are ungrateful and disrespectful to their elders, mainly their parents. Humans can be raised to a very wise understanding of life and our base desires leads us to a profane and foolish outlook on living. I think we, as in humans, should recognize our traits which are worthy of reverence and acknowledge our habits than makes us seem lower than animals.

I wonder if they noticed that they're the only species who cloak
    their nakedness,
Every since our primordial parents decided to taste of the fruits of
    the tree of wisdom and knowledge,
In result they learned the pain of understanding,
We're the only species so animalistic in desire that we must cover
    our beastly shame,
The product of despised juices,
When emitted in the earth,
She immediately cleanse her womb of the smell of it's traces,
Even the birthstone that provides these waters of life purifies its self
    of its scent,
The seed nurtures in the soil with the assistance of the sustenance
    provided by the Sun and springs,
Behold it blossoms,
With its roots firm and branches stretched dispersing leaves, fruits,
    and colors of in return it curses the earth, sun and springs
    that fostered it,
Such strange fruit,
Justly it grows old and with age loses all of its splendor and lustre,
It returns back to its infantile state,
Once again it needs to be supported with weaning,
Yet old and despised it finds no one attentive to its needs for
    suckling,
As the sword of time does everyone,
It cuts off its existence of-life on this plane,
Plunged into an perpetuallity of nothingness,
Not even pondered by all the containers of vessels of memories
    that it left behind.

Halim A. Flowers

Death

*I was in solitary confinement (the hole) when I was inspired to write this.
The hole is racially segregated; Afrikan descent people are isolated from
every other ethnic group. This division suggest that Afrikans are the
enemies. The tension is so thick you can smell it. My thoughts were of
death. The people in the hole were generating that type of energy.*

I open my eyes every morning returning from a form of death,
Breathing a breath that will bring me one breath closer to death,
I pray to prepare myself for what awaits in the state of death,
Fearing a torment in where there is neither life nor death,
I consume the good sustenance to prevent myself from an
    unhealthy death,
I look out at the two cells across from me and see pale and brown
    faces who for geographical reasons are seeking my death,
I hear the officers of correction putting on helmets and other
    equipment to beat a Man to death,
On the bunk underneath lies a man who meditates on the revenge
    for lost love plotting the perpetrators death,
I hear the hopeless ones down the hall talking about their
    excapades of sodomistic pleasures though I'm aware their
    making love with death,
I call my sister to hear tales of the club and popping bottles to
    swallow death,
Then talk to my mother to be informed my brother has distorted
    his sanity because of his desire to inhale death,
My dearest love, my heart, my door to existence has found solace
    in a companion whose entangled in a matrimonial bond and
    everything I live on says that they're worthy of death,
I look at a vent in this cell and a remnant of a string remains where
    a desperate male hung himself to death
I read in the newspaper where all of the leaders on earth say the
    only way to peace is to war with death,

All those who are breathing are deceived to think they are living
   but the ignorant are only an existence of death,
Even me with all my grand plans to remove injustice from the land,
   will probably lead to my death,
Even though we are surrounded by it, the cretins are the ones who
   encase their hearts with fear of death.

The Streets

I wrote this about the streets. It was inspired by a letter from my young sister Angie.

Even though your in the club,
You're still in the streets,
You don't have to be a thug to have love for the streets,
Everybody in a cell wants to go back to the streets,
Persistent reminiscence about what they did on the streets,
She has opened her legs to a chosen few so she doesn't feel that
    she's a freak,
She desires much so she decides to become an entrepreneur on
    the streets,
In the car with her man being stopped by the cops he hands her
    the gun and says,
"Take this Beef",
Stunned she replies, "huh",
He counters, "Don't you know the roll of a whore in the streets",
The hearts of men are cold and bold on the streets,
So Lil Man never leaves the house without his heat,
So one day Lil Man and his comrade was chillin on the streets,
Lil Man comrade got into a scuffle and Lil Man caught a body
    beef,
Detectives question his comrade and he decides to give a speech,
Damn Lil Man you knew but failed to tell your comrade the code
    of the streets,
Everybody in this world is searching for peace,
A few good men are resting in it sacrificed by the streets,
Like a black hole in the galaxy it's a gravatational pull in the
    streets,
Make a muslim sell crack with a kufi on,
As Salamu Alaikum I'm just trying to get on my feet,
Don't even try to look no more because aint nothing good in the
    streets,
You still occupy them though,
Simple fact is that you're weak,
Off to college to receive a degree and five languages she speaks,

Can't wait until summer break so she can run in the streets,
One of his brothers died there and the other one snatched by the
    feds in a sweep,
With all those thorns surrounding it he is still hugging the streets,
You say that you've kicked that habit for 3 weeks,
But still enshroud yourself with attics from the streets,
A cage and a early grave are two best friends of the streets,
And sometimes a wheelchair,
You'll still roll that on the streets,
Live by the streets,
Die in the streets,
What make you rich can make you cry because of the streets.

No Explanations

I wrote this for my young sister Angie. It is hard to advise those I care about from this U.S. Oppression System. Society is like a game of chess, you can see it better when you are a spectator but make foolish moves when you're playing.

What can I actually say to her?
How could she possibly accept me telling her to slow down?
While she walks upon my former tracks and can still smell my skid
    marks,
How could I explain to her that it is more fruitful to plant a tree
    instead of smoking leaves?
Does it seem respectable for me to lecture her about the pearls of
    peace when it took for me to be isolated from her world to
    even begin to grasp it's branches?
How can I explain to her the importance of studying history?
When she still hears the dead glorify my shotgun charades,
How can I teach her the sublimity of the womb?
When I was once known to boast about beating it up,
How can I show her that her children will be the liberators of the
    neopenal colonies?
How can I explain to her how important she is to the survival of my
    people by?
Writing her wisdom which she studies for her short stay in her
    abode but walks out her door to a world that only sees her for
    how much flesh she possesses in her bra strap and denim?
What can I really say to her?

Exalted

This was inspired by one of the most militant and brilliant comrades that I've ever met. No matter how much I learn, the brother seems to find a way to send me back to the books. Every person needs somebody that inspire them. And then we must be humble enough to accept their admonition.

I guess every era, every community, every family, and comrade has an Ali,
Someone who has been sent into our environment to pull up even
      those who are grounded,
An individual who is manifested in our presence to remind us that
      we still have much to learn,
And to secretly inform us that we are not as sublime as we often
      hold ourselves to be,
He can come in the form of a teacher, a brother, a comrade, a co-
      defendant, and many other appearances,
Some of us have him with us and are too defiant to recognize and
      accept that someone is above our self-conceived perfect intellect,
Even Moses couldn't be patient with the elevated understanding of Khidr,
So I've learned that hasteness and inattentiveness could cause a
      severe departure of that vessel of brilliance,
Every Ali has an Ali,
And it all reverts back to the One,
Some of us exalt ourselves and don't realize that exaltation comes
      from adhering to the ones who are exalted,
And their exaltation comes from submitting to The Exalted,
Whoever your Ali may be,
Make your conscious a sponge for his words of wisdom,
Accept his defects,
And honor his dignity,
I feel better because my Ali without intent has instructed me that
      there are people better than myself,
And with that revelation I know humility,
We all need an Ali to remind us that we are human,
Recognize your Exalted person
Your Ali!

Lion Tears

During my incarceration, I've met inmates who were in solitary confinement in Marion Penitentiary in the 80's and other brothers who fought in Vietnam. Another brother told me about the racism he experienced in Marion as tears fell from his face. Another older brother explained the trauma of fighting in Vietnam and he would just start crying like a child. I can't imagine how it feels to fight for your sovereignty in alien territory and later in your life be incarcerated by the same rulers whom you've shed your sanity for.

What they saw I can't explain,
Two different places but their struggles and tears are the same,
In the jungles of Vietnam in the 60's and 70's,
And Marion Penitentiary in the 80's,
I hear their tales of seeing death and paranoia of always facing it,
Not being afraid but prepared even in their sleep for the
    exploding land mine, the
Viet Russian rifle touting man-child popping out of the unseen
    underground tunnel,
The shank taped to the broomstick through the bars, or the
    homemade pop-gun with 38 shells,
Souls immune to living with their comrade yesterday and seeing
    him mowed down by machine guns or his genitals cut off and
    placed in his mouth and body butchered by the sharp edge of
    the tip of today,
From the "Black Man Go Home" signs, war time frontline
    discrimination, the guards taking their weapons and giving
    them to their enemies who'd come to their bars offering a gift
    of fatal recreation,
They both saw the hatred and bloody casualties of racism in its
    most treacherous form,
Two tales,
Two jungles,
One with trees and grass,
And the other concrete and steel,
Both drenched with memories of hate and blood,
Whose survival produced lions,

I listen to those old lions narrate their tales of horror,
And as those strong thorough dangerous veterans of those wars
recall their torments,
They shed tears which I drink to quench my thirst for the wisdom
of the past.

3-17-03

This is a protest against the many frivolous avenues of entertainment that many people cherish and worship. We hold in very high esteem these various amusements but show no enthusiasm towards the people and things that are making life more peaceful for creation. Some of us devout more attention to music videos, movies, sporting events, and etc., than we invest uplifting the consciousness and conditions of ourselves.

Why should I be elated in madness by the sight of a ball in a basket
    in March?
For surely I've witnessed greater events,
Like the release of Nelson Mandela from unjust captivity,
The homeless lady feeding the birds,
The protrait of Elian and Assata in Cuba,
A mother giving suck to her offspring,
The librarian who reads to the children,
The son washing and kissing the feet, combing the hair and
    keeping the house of his elderly mother,
The volunteer serving food at the shelter,
Why do people enrich the politicians and judges with praises and
    gifts?
And make the teachers and doctors protest and strike for better
    wages,
It is like the tree growing to make rules to annoy and curse it's root
Engrossed in frivolous traditions
We become clouded from the purest precious thoughts, sights, and
    moments.

Freedom

This is a constitution of freedom. Sort of a script for my own Utopia. I want to be free from any image, voice, touch, or thought that will disturb my peace of self.

Free from fear and its contributing elements,
Free from oppression, injustice and ignorance,
Free from the hand of the thief,
Free from the possibility of the molestation of children,
Free from the perverts raping our women,
Free from racial hatred,
Free from lies,
Freed from the images of families separated by indifferences,
Free from thirst and hunger,
Free from purchasing natural elements like water,
Free from intentional and unwarranted violence,
Free from poverty,
Freed from rich and poor,
Free from man selling and claiming ownership of earth that he
    didn't create,
Free from jealousy and envy,
Freed from witnessing the homeless,
Free from cures being unaffordable for the ill,
Freed from selfishness and greed,
Freed from illegitimate relations,
With this freedom we will enjoy peace,
And comprehend and sincerely show love.

Retro

I wrote this for my big sister who never backs down. You are special to me.

Chocolate Chip Ice Cream,
Listening to Anita Baker sing about Mysteries,
Mother of Fudge,
Ebony Exotic complexion,
With an ivory smile,
Always ready for spaghetti,
Never ran from a fight,
Conscious enough to vibe with Erykah Badu and The Wu,
A well of untapped revolutionary and activist spirits,
Ready to explode and flood the grounded with insurrectionist
    nurturing,
Although rooted in different lands,
We are forever tied to the blood of the loins of the husbandman,
You had to be tough to tolerate, handle, and put fear in a little bad
    ass brother like me,
But you managed,
Plus survived your parents rapid decay from addiction in your
    youth,
It's impossible to believe you're weak,
And you must give birth to the strong.

The Effect

This was written about the most intelligent woman that I've ever met in this life, Anissa. The sister has assisted me in my development as a man and these words are a declaration of the feelings that she generates.

She makes the unattainable seem accomplishable,
For the hard answers she hears simple questions,
She is the professor of the hearts of the wise men,
Savant attend her school to obtain a Master's life,
The tyro gets hazed by the smack of her intelligence,
The sober become intoxicated when they sip a dose of her reality,
She makes the strong even stronger and feel weak at the same
    time,
Her womb gives birth to insurrection,
Her breasts contain the liquid of revolution,
She possesses a sea of knowledge that the cretins
    find hard to swim in,
Her lap is the root of every activist,
She was born with the keys to the treasure of sanity and peace.

Halim A. Flowers

Distantly Close

I wrote this about a relationship between a man incarcerated and a woman in society. In this poem, I attempted to see the relationship from both points of views. I understand that every woman is not Winnie Mandela.

Never knew that I could love someone so intense that it would be
    awkward to just be their friend,
Your images gives birth to thoughts that soothe my sanity,
We've accepted each others fables
And blindly ran into the brick wall of each others deceptive
    excuses,
We've been tested by deceit, separation, and distrust,
So now all that's left is for us to walk away forever from our broken
    glass,
Or to grow in the union of peace and love,
Lay a foundation of honesty upon the soil of understanding,
And slide along the grains of sand through the tube of life in the
    hour glass
To be deferential about our differences,
Learn that we both are amateurs in the profession of life,
Still my selfishness block my senses of seeing my captivity from your
    vision,
Your natural cravings of just wanting to touch, smell, hear, and
    taste me,
Surely the internal tears from your emotional strain far outweighed
    my desire for you to isolate yourself from the norm of
    breathing,
Who am I to ask you to incarcerate yourself from society,
Who am I to ask you to incarcerate yourself from society,
And cage yourself into my present world of loneliness.

So Your Going To Kill Me

A good brother who goes by the name of C-Dog, and I to wrote poems spontaneously without preparing. So this is what was communicated to my fingertips and pen.

I understand that out of your torpidity that you
You'll let them cuff you,
And I just bumped you,
So your going to kill me,
They tell you to remove your laces and confiscate your shoes,
I accidently step on them and sincerely apologize,
So your going to kill me,
They separated you from your family indefinitely,
And I was just making one 15 minute call
So your going to kill me,
They've been taking taxes from your mother for illusory and
      unattainable benefits,
I just owe you fifty dollars,
So your going to kill me,
The locale of their exalted sovereign, dome of oppressive
      legislation, and suite of the chief of their nation,
Although the soil of my upbringing, I never aligned with the
      wicked communion,
So your going to kill me,
They defame you, strip you, chain you, whip you,
All I did was enlighten you about that issue,
So your going to kill me,
Is it I who opposes you on that indictment,
Prowl over the barrier of your freedom with the intent and means
      to eliminate you if you step within reach,
Did I deny you a passionate touch, a consoling voice?
I'm staring at the edge of your sword, the barrel of your choice of
      destruction,
My bone felt the pain of your rage,
Would you care if I showed you that you are aiding and abetting
      the enemy of yourself?
So Your Going To Kill Me?

Halim A. Flowers

Respect Is Due

I wrote this for my Afrikan people who endured the trials of American slavery. For some reason, the males in this country have loss the respect and consciousness of the immeasurable value of our females. Our sisters have stuck with us through so much. Although, she may be lacking the knowledge of her precious, unique, and extraordinary self, she still commands and deserve admiration. Just out of reverence for all of the strong and loyal Afrikan women that she has descended from.

Respect to the earth is due;
As we allowed her to be shackled and chained;
She still honored us as like kings;
As we were subjected to barbaric savagery and humiliation;
She consoled us in native Afrikan tongue that, "it'll be alright";
When we cowardly watched when our captors invaded our shacks
    and raped our queens before our eyes;
Somehow she still managed to acknowledge us as men;
Birthed sons with the oppressors blood but still loved them;
No matter how many times the baas mortified us and annihilated
    our Integrity as men;
She never refused us her womb for the cultivation of our seeds;
Nurtured and weaned in slave ships, plantations, sheds, projects,
    and prisons;
Stuck with us through slavery, jim crow, and life sentences;
The responder of prison letters;
Our visitor while in bondage;
There hasn't been a lynching, beating, burnt cross or death row
    potent enough to fracture our bond;
I don't care if she is sexually loose or dons the attire of a harlot;
Even if I see her in the club or deteriating from drugs;
She is the receptor of my illumination;
The soil for my seed;
The Harriet Tubman that rescues me from my plantation of
    loneliness;
The queen of my soul;
Her essence demands the recognition as such;
Respect is due!

D' Juan

This is a message to a fallen comrade who was unfortunate to be denied the chance to exist. While in society, I was his mentor and mislead him, and to learn of his death, produced an energy of failure and guilt. I didn't strive hard enough to establish communication with him when I became awakened from my long repose.

From my cage I called to you;
But the frivilities of society were loud enough to block my plea;
I just wanted to let you know that I saw where you going;
I failed you little brother;
I should have screamed louder so that you could feel me;
These bars are not strong enough to imprison the truth;
Maybe if I would've explained the struggle of Nat Turner,
    Jonathan, George Jackson, Marcus Garvey, and Denmark
    Vescey, you would've destroyed the snare that was set for your
    demise;
But the possibilities of "IF" are just merely that, POSSIBILITIES;
Whether it is the bullet or the bars;
A blueprint and means of its execution has been devised to make
    us die;
And to make your mother and father cry;
Whether we're being lowered in the earth;
Or condemned to an existence of inhumane captivity;
Either way we experience or live death;
And all of our family and comrades wither away with us;
Little brother your demise is worth a million tears;
So now you join me in the world of memories;
Remembered only by words, thoughts, experiences, and
    photographs;
But young warrior I won't allow the world to forget you, Chip, or
    Shawn;

Halim A. Flowers

For you I shed tears of blood upon our ancestors souls;
Life is an university and death presents its testes;
So wherever your essence may now exist;
Rest and learn the lesson of it all;

In Peace;

Love Halim

Somebody Better Cry for Me

I wrote this poem explaining that I've witnessed so much destruction and oppression, that I can't cry. In light of this reality, somebody please cry for me.

I've been separated from all that I was taught to love;
Family, friends, and a choice;
A choice to eat, sleep, and bathe;
I've been stripped searched naked of my common privacies;
A Human;
A man of hue held captive by ghost;
In a zoo in which the animals trains and maintains the people;
I've been purged with humiliation until now my soul is dry;
Somebody better cry for me;
In modest weeping is dignity but I can't build up the courage for
     tears;
Locked-up, locked-down, wrists and ankles cuffed from left to
     right;
No proms, graduations, weddings, honeymoons or baby showers;
Somebody better cry for me;
The mirror of my soul needs to secrete some tension;
But the bitter years enshrouded by concrete and steel has absorbed
     my liquid of pain;
My heart has became a freezing desert;
Frigid and vapid;
Beatings, isolation, suicides, mayhem, religious fanatics, rapes,
     exhibitionism;
Loneliness and mandated abstinence;
If I could produce the emotion to rain on my face I'd flood the
     earth;
But I can't;
Somebody Better Cry For Me!!!

Halim A. Flowers

A Reason to Breathe

I wrote this poem because I believe most people suffer from stress and depression because they don't have a reason to breathe. Therefore, they don't find any enjoyment in living. Life without purpose is useless. If we truly desire peace then establishing a reason for living will make the task of maintaining our sanity much easier.

To make my mother a grandma is a reason to Breathe;
To make a woman my queen is a reason to Breathe;
The attempt to uplift my people is a reason to Breathe;
Liberation from incarceration is a reason to Breathe;
Watching Babylon falling is a reason to Breathe;
The destruction of economic classes of society is a reason to
    Breathe;
Vengeance of my ancestors blood is a reason to Breathe;
Revolution against oppression is a reason to Breathe;
What is life without a reason to live but misery
Everybody needs a reason to Breathe.

A

REASON

TO

BREATHE

THE SONG

Halim A. Flowers

THE SONG

HOOK
Shorties with HIV;
Need a reason to breathe;
Youngins that's counting gees;
Need a reason to breathe;
My people up in the bing;
Need a reason to breathe;
They need a reason to breathe;

My people up in the hood;
Need a reason to breathe;
When stuff ain't looking good;
Need a reason to breathe;
Resort to laying wood;
Need a reason to breathe;
They need a reason to breathe;

VERSE 1

by Halim Flowers

VERSE 1

Some people living life with no purpose; Constant visits to the psyche doctor and counseling just aint working; Gun in their mouth trying to figure out if it's worth it; Others found God inside of themselves instead of the churches; A 40 ounce to a drunk is a reason to breathe; Billionares finding a reason to breathe; When I stress I retrieve; Read George Jackson letters and listen to Dead Prez cause the revolution is a reason for me; To keep exercising keep writing and keep rhyming; Deep lessons manifested in life force me to keep striving; Can't knock what maintains the strain on the brain; as long as it's not methadone heroin or cocaine; novacaine the pain is numb it's strange that some do the same as them; But yet they steady blaming them; I refrain from them box fake akhees out of my cipher; Most of them thespians like Mekhi Pheifer.

VERSE 2

by Daru Swinton

VERSE 2

To stay alive that's my reason to breathe; I'm going all out taking
off like when the cops told me to freeze; I got nothing to lose alot
to gain; So if I die I'm still living only thing missing is my physical
frame; But while I'm here I m loving everything coming my way; I
take the bitter with the sweet I went from shallow to deep; Ignorant
to conscious black wise guys at the conference; Never talk nonsense
we correspond intelligent comments; The Creator's creation
creating a reason to breathe; Especially my kind I call us the
melanin breed; Experienced the gutters the lower levels with high
spirits; My soul navigates for my body and my mind steers it; My
moms hears it the struggle in my voice "Boo you alright"; To make
the righteous choice is truly my plight; Day and night the sun and
moon take their post I see it; I get a chill inside cause in my mind I
know I exceed it; On some earth twist shit Fuck talking bout
cooking a brick up; Its mind over matter this whole game I'm
trying to lift up; Like Biggie Pac and Pun did to them give big ups;
A Reason To Breathe even in book stores something to pick up.

REPEAT THE HOOK ...

HOOK
Shorties with HIV;
Need a reason to breathe;
Youngins that's counting gees;
Need a reason to breathe;
My people up in the bing;
Need a reason to breathe;
They need a reason to breathe;

My people up in the hood;
Need a reason to breathe;
When stuff ain't looking good;
Need a reason to breathe;
Resort to laying wood;
Need a reason to breathe;
They need a reason to breathe;

P.S.

First of all, I would like to thank God for inspiring me with thought and assisting me in my expressions. Also, I would like to send my love and appreciation to my Mother, Father, Brother, Sister, Pup (My Other Mother), Mema, Stephanie, Anissa (Let's Do A Book Together), Angela (Lis Sis), Pug (Co-D), Kareem (Islam), Jesse, Zay, Timika (Slow Down!), Naeem, C-Dog (Keep Rolling), Daru (Hollis!), Ali, Abdul-Hakeem, Malachi, Muhammad Adbullah, Big George, Boo (What's Up Cousin), Bumpy (Thanks For Giving Me Soledad Brother To Read), Ashanta (My Grandfather), my family, comrades, and all those who inspire me to live and think better.

Special thanks to Lawrence Hill Books,
Myron Briggs and Clarke Allen.

Contact the Author:
Halim A. Flowers (11967-007)
USP
P.O. Box 1000
Lewisburg, PA 17837